VICTORIAN
PRESERVES, PICKLES,
AND
RELISHES

POTTER/CLARKSON PUBLISHERS NEW YORK

AUTHENTIC
TREATS,
RECIPES, AND
CUSTOMS FROM
AMERICA'S
BYGONE
ERA

APPLE BUTTER

CATNIP

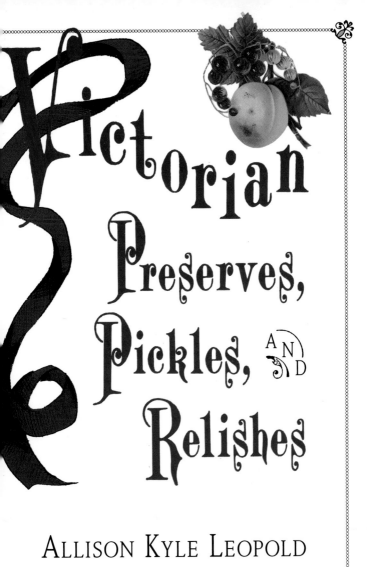

Victorian Preserves, Pickles, and Relishes

ALLISON KYLE LEOPOLD

RESEARCH CONSULTANT:
JOANNE LEONHARDT CASSULLO

Published by Clarkson N. Potter, Inc., 201 East 50th Street, New York,
New York 10022. Member of the Crown Publishing Group.

CLARKSON N. POTTER, POTTER and colophon are trademarks of
Clarkson N. Potter, Inc.

Manufactured in Japan
Design by Beth Tondreau Design/Mary A. Wirth

Library of Congress Cataloging-in-Publication Data
Leopold, Allison Kyle.
Victorian preserves, pickles, and relishes: authentic treats, recipes, and
customs from America's bygone era/Allison Kyle Leopold. — 1st ed.
p.   cm.
1. Jam.   2. Pickles.   3. Cookery (Relishes)   4. England — Social life
and customs — 19th century.   I. Title.
TX612.J3L56   1992
614.4'09034 — dc20
91–46160
CIP

ISBN 0-517-58315-1
10 9 8 7 6 5 4 3 2 1
First Edition

CONTENTS

❦

INTRODUCTION · 7

1 · PRESERVES · 13
Plum and Apple Jam . . . Strawberries
Peach Butter . . . Crystallized Fruit
Fruit Glacé . . . Iced Pineapple . . . Iced Fruits
Brandied Fruit

2 · PICKLES · 31
Mixed Pickle
Watermelon and Sweet Ginger Pickles
Tomato Mangoes . . . Blue-Berry Pickles
Sweet Pickle for Fruit

3 · RELISHES · 47
Kate's Lily Pickle . . . Peach Catsup
ChowChow (Superior English Recipe)
Green Grape Chutney . . . Plum Catsup

PROCESSING AND CANNING · 56
THE PROPER TIME TO CAN
FRUITS AND VEGETABLES · 59
GLOSSARY · 60
ACKNOWLEDGMENTS · 64

INTRODUCTION

Equipped with silver knife and enamelled preserving
kettle, the housewife joyously proceeds with her task of
converting the baskets or cases of luscious fruit into
delicious preserves, spicy, pungent pickles, rich
marmalades and translucent jellies; and when
all is finished, it is with worthy pride and
satisfaction that she gazes upon the
"fruits of her labor."
—"The Housekeeper," THE LADIES' WORLD, 1901

One of the distinguishing characteristics of the
Victorian table was the array of condiments,
both savory and sweet, that accompanied every
meal. Rich, mushroom - flavored catsups, spicy
chowchows, Indian pickle, and colorful piccalilli gave
flavor and variety to everyday meats and fish, while
fruit-laden preserves dressed up nutty breads or
biscuits at tea.

Simple necessity made these condiments popular:
pickling and preserving fruits and vegetables at the
height of their season, usually summer and early fall,
were among the limited ways to ensure a supply of

produce throughout the year. Before the days of reliable refrigeration and other convenient techniques, foods were routinely smoked, dried, potted, pickled, and preserved. These tasks were not difficult, but they were time-consuming; kettles simmered on the cookstove from July through November.

One South Dakota woman, in an account of her prairie girlhood during the 1880s, recalled returning from school to the syrupy scent of preserves and the spicy odor of pickles, as her mother made preserves from the red tomatoes, purple husk tomatoes, and golden ground-cherries that the girl and her sisters had gathered, and pickles from the green tomatoes that would not have time to ripen. These chores of pickling and preserving were but part of the routine pattern of Victorian domestic life. The letters of Elinore Pruitt Stewart, a homesteader in Wyoming in 1909, also recall the task: "I have done most of my cooking at night, have milked seven cows every day, have done all the hay-cutting, so you see I have been working. But I have found time to put up thirty pints of jelly and the same amount of jam for myself. I used wild fruits, gooseberries, currants, raspberries, and cherries. I have almost two gallons of cherry butter, and I think it is delicious. I wish I could get some of it to·you. I am sure you would like it."

Relishes like chopped pepper pickle and condiments like green grape chutney and peach or walnut catsup relieved the monotony of the nineteenth-century table, allowing families to enjoy the novelty of fruits and vegetables out of season. Chokecherry jam and gooseberry chutney, sparkling in pressed-glass dishes, filled many a country Victorian supper table, while the fad for fashionable pickles reached such proportions during the 1860s and early 1870s that magazines began to condemn it. Schoolgirls were particularly devoted, and columnist Jenny June, writing in *Demorest's Monthly Magazine* (1873), noted such teenage "food fancies." "When girls have entered their teens, they begin to be subject to fancies about their food," she wrote, mentioning the "vulgar" slate, lead-pencil, and pickle manias, the last of which had "about died out." Readers of Louisa May Alcott's *Little Women*, will no doubt remember schoolgirl Amy's mouth-watering purchase of two dozen moist and delicious pickled limes.

Cupboard shelves and pantries lined with carefully labeled jars of pickled vegetables, relishes, jams, and jellies were tangible symbols of a woman's domestic prowess, the sweet and savory fruits of her labor. Cookery guides painstakingly provided careful instructions for both pickling and preserving, and much feminine discussion revolved around discovering the best and most efficient methods. *The Household,* a popular magazine of the 1880s, provided a forum for readers to share their receipts, as recipes were known, with their "sisters." In September 1880, Mrs. Harry Baker wrote, "I have in my possession a recipe for canning rhubarb which I tried last year, but failed completely, and I wish to ask my many sisters if they have ever tried it, and were they successful?" She also asked for directions for "putting down" cucumber pickles in vinegar without salting them first. "Pearlwood asks how to make strawberry preserves," began one *Household* column. "We like our strawberry jam very much and perhaps she might like the recipe." Another *Household* column commented, "Although too late for some of the small fruits, the season for peaches, plums, quinces, etc., is just com-

mencing, and perhaps a few hints in regard to the preserving of such for winter use, may be of some interest to the less experienced readers of *The Household* of which — especially since our editor's generous offer to brides — there must be not a few."

July began the push to begin preserving abundant summer fruits like raspberries, and cherries; in the fall, apples, pears, and even walnuts were "put by." Cooks selected and handled their fruit carefully. "No imperfect fruit should be canned or preserved," said the author of *Canned Fruit, Preserves and Jellies: Household Methods of Preparation* (1904).

Today there is renewed interest in these old-fashioned specialties that lent such distinction to Victorian dining. Savory mushroom-flavored catsup (easily the most popular catsup flavor during the nineteenth century) turns a simple roast into a lively entrée; brandied, spiced, and frosted fruits are easy but special accompaniments to desserts; and homemade jams, jellies, and preserves are richer in flavor than their commercial equivalents. While customs and technologies have changed (the recipes here, while authentic, have been annotated to accommodate those changes), the delights of Victorian cookery are just being rediscovered. A few jars from the cupboard provide a taste of the table of long ago.

CHAPTER

1

Preserves

Although the word preserves is most commonly used today to denote a thick jam, made from fruit, during the nineteenth century it referred to a wide range of both fruit *and* vegetable preparations. Berry preserves, jams, and jellies were among the most popular, but green tomato jelly and pumpkin preserves were also favorites. *The Household Magazine* (1881) distinguished between jam and marmalade as follows:

> To Aunt Abbie who asks in the July number the difference between jam and marmalade, I would say that marmalade is sifted, cooked longer than jam, and if properly made is smooth and firm enough to cut with a knife.

Jam is soft like any preserve, except that the fruit is mashed and stirred to a smooth mass, instead of leaving it whole. There is also less sugar used in most jam than in marmalade and preserves. Berries, pineapples, peaches, plums and grapes make the best jam; quinces, oranges and apples, the best marmalade. Apples make a very nice foundation for marmalades, flavoring with other fruits. One large pineapple, or two or three quinces, (or the peelings and cores of the latter, left from preserves), to half a peck of apples, makes it very nice.

The realm of preserves also included spiced and brandied fruits, as well as fruits that were frosted, crystallized or glacéed. Frozen glacéed oranges were a particular favorite of cookery expert Marion Harland, who found them "especially refreshing in hot weather."

Finally, Victorian fruit and nut butters were also considered preserves of a kind. For example, *The American Housewife Cookbook* (1880), by Miss T. S. Shute, offered the following simple receipt for hazelnut butter under that category: "Scald and blanch some hazel nuts; pound them to a paste in a mortar, adding gradually a small quantity of butter. This is good to eat with wild fowl or to flavor the most delicate sauces."

SPICED PLUMS

Take firm, ripe plums, prick the skins with a darning needle and put them in a jar. To one quart of vinegar allow three pounds of sugar, one ounce of ground cloves, one ounce of cinnamon. Make a syrup and pour boiling hot over the plums. Seal immediately.

—"Household Topics,"
THE LADIES' WORLD, 1901

A great many of the fruit preserves that graced the Victorian table were meant to be served with meat, fish, or fowl. Barberry (also called berberry) preserves were considered a delicious addition to venison, winged game, or roast turkey. Spiced or pickled grapes were enjoyed—"particularly good," said *The Ladies' World* (1901)—when served with game or cold meats. Wild grapes, if procurable, were said to be the best. According to *The Mayflower* (1896), green apple preserves "if rightly done" were equal to an East Indian preserve.

Preserves, jams, jellies, and marmalades were also accepted as sweets. One of the most popular ways to serve fruit preserves was to spread them between cake layers, and bread and jam was a treat that children clamored for well into the twentieth century.

The Household Magazine (1881) advised putting aside the syrup saved in making preserves—"a delicious syrup for hot cakes during the winter." And preserved oranges, beautifully clear and almost transparent, "form a delightful dish, either whole or halved, and filled with orange jelly at the time of serving," *The Mayflower Magazine* told its readers in the 1890s. Sliced in rings, oranges made a lovely garnish for fancy dishes, while the syrup was a delicious addition to sauces and popular Victorian desserts like Bavarian cream.

Victorians sought the perfect fruit—sound and free of defects—and picked it just prior to ripeness. Cooks preferred white sugar to brown sugar or molasses. Fruit was put up in stone jars or crocks, but in 1881 *The Household of the Detroit Free Press,* while still favoring stone jars, also mentioned glass. *The White House Cook Book,* speaking from the lofty vantage point of 1887, when sterilized canning methods had begun to revolutionize even home techniques, pointed out that now effective preserving required less sugar—not pound for pound, as in "the old days."

The Victorians were also concerned with how to seal their preserves to keep them from spoiling. "Mold can be prevented from forming on fruit jellies by pouring a little melted paraffine over the top," *The*

White House Cook Book pointed out. "When cool, it will harden to a solid cake which can be easily removed when the jelly is used, and saved to use over again another year. It is perfectly harmless and tasteless." In 1880 Maria Parloa recommended self-sealing glass jars with rubber rings or bands "to keep fruit for years," while her jellies and jams went into tumblers or bowls topped with brandied paper. Other safeguards to prevent fermentation included sealing jars with buttered paper (alone or topped with a layer of salt brine), parchment, a snugly fitted pig's bladder, cork and sealing wax, a thick layer of sugar, clarified mutton fat, or warm salad oil. One method guaranteed to be foolproof called for placing a thick layer of cotton batting on top of brandied writing paper or manila paper to keep the jar airtight. *The Household Magazine* (1880) favored covering jars with white tissue paper dipped in egg white (a popular choice, repeated in other periodicals as well). *The Household of the Detroit Free Press* offered the following variation: one layer of paper dipped in salad oil, with tissue paper brushed in egg white stretched on top.

Most of these methods are primitive compared to our refined processes of today. See "Processing and Canning" (page 56) rather than risk contamination of the delightful preserves on the following pages.

PLUM AND APPLE JAM

After canning plums, there is often some left, not enough to fill a can; a very nice jam can be made of this by putting it through a sieve, and adding the same quantity of good apples, cooked. Sweeten to taste, and put in a very little cinnamon and cloves. Cook an hour, then tie up in jars when cold.

—Mrs. T. J. Kirkpatrick,
THE HOUSEKEEPER'S NEW COOK BOOK, 1883

NOTE: This mix of two Victorian favorites is particularly nice on tea biscuits or homemade bread. Prepare jars as directed on page 57. It is not necessary to put the plums through a sieve. Use 2 pounds brandied pitted plums (see "To Brandy All Kinds of Fruit," page 28), 2 pounds cored, peeled, and diced Granny Smith apples, 2 cups sugar, 1 teaspoon cinnamon, and 1 teaspoon cloves. Cook over medium heat for 5 minutes, or until the fruit is slightly softened. Bring to a boil, uncovered, then reduce the heat to low and simmer for 1½ to 2 hours, or until thick, stirring occasionally. Pour the hot jam into the jars to within ¼ inch of the rim. Seal and process for 15 minutes as directed on pages 56–58.

Makes 6 cups.

STRAWBERRIES

To each pound of berries allow half a pound of sugar. Put the berries in a kettle, and mash them a little, so that there will be juice enough to cook them without using water. Stir them to prevent scorching. Cook fifteen minutes; then add the sugar, and let them boil hard one minute. Put them in the jars as directed. More or less sugar may be used, as one prefers.

VARIATIONS: *Raspberries* To each pound of berries allow three-fourths of a pound of sugar, and cook the same as the strawberries. *Currants* Currants should be prepared the same as raspberries.

—Maria Parloa,
MISS PARLOA'S NEW COOK BOOK, 1880

NOTE: Berries prepared this way can be served spooned over cake or ice cream. Prepare jars as directed on page 57. Use 4 cups of berries, washed, hulled, and dried, and stir over medium-low heat for 45 minutes to 1 hour, or until thick. Fill the jars to within ½ to ¼ inch of the rim. Seal and process for 15 minutes as directed on pages 56–58. Refrigerate after opening.
  Makes about 3 cups.

PEACH BUTTER

To every pound of peaches, weighed after peeling and stoning, allow one-half pound of sugar. Pare and stone the peaches, which should be very ripe and mellow; cut in pieces and put through the press. Put over the fire in a porcelain kettle; let the pulp heat slowly and cook, stirring occasionally, until it is of the consistency of marmalade. Add the sugar, stir until it is dissolved and cook rapidly for fifteen minutes. Place the kettle on the back part of the stove, where the butter will not become cooled until it is quite solid. Pack in jars or tumblers while hot.

—Helen Louise Johnson,
THE ENTERPRISING HOUSEKEEPER, 1898

NOTE: This sweet spread resembles a cross between a fruit butter and a jam. Prepare jars as directed on page 57. Use 2 pounds peaches and 2 cups sugar. A blender or food processor can be used instead of a press. For a smoother texture, strain through a sieve. Simmer over low heat for 1½ to 2 hours, or until thick. Fill the jars to within ¼ inch of the rim. Seal and process for 15 minutes as directed on pages 56–58. Refrigerate after opening.

Makes 3 cups.

Large fruit such as peaches, pears, etc., are in the best condition to can when not quite fully ripe and should be put up as soon as possible after picking. Small fruit, such as berries, should never stand overnight if it is possible to avoid it. Use only the best sugar in the proportion of half a pound to a pound of fruit, varying the rule, of course, with the sweetness of the fruit.

—May Perrin Goff,

The Household of the Detroit Free Press, 1881

To Crystallize Any Fruit That Will Keep Its Form; Also Nuts

Make a syrup of one cup of sugar, four tablespoonfuls of water and two of vinegar; when it boils stir in a small pinch of soda; stir as little as possible, or the candy will not be clear; boil till it hairs. . . . Separate the fruit from the stems; grapes, cherries, oranges (whose quarters have been separated about twenty-four hours beforehand, to become dry and hard), cutting out the seeds carefully, so the juice will not escape; citron cut in pretty forms; dip each fruit or piece of nut in the warm syrup, and lay it on waxed paper in a cool place to harden. If the first dipping is not successful go over the operation again, adding a little more water to the syrup, and when it stands the test, dip again. Syrup can be worked over twelve times in case of a failure of fruit crystallizing. Use granulated sugar. Don't stir syrup after it comes to a boil. If your syrup should candy, add a little more water and sugar, and just as it is coming to a boil drop in a pinch of cream of tartar to the quantity of syrup described; this will prevent it from candying. Use the same remedy in making candies.

N.B. Six drops of lemon juice may be used instead of the cream of tartar.

— Patented and Improved Methods of
  Preserving and Canning Fruits, Vegetables, etc.,
  Also Pickling Fruits and Vegetables, 1890

Note: Victorian cooks often used terms like *frosted, glacéed, iced,* and *candied* in different ways. The glossary on pages 60–62 gives general definitions. Fruits and nuts that can be beautifully crystallized in this manner include cherries, grapes, plums, apricots, kumquats, orange sections, and walnuts and chestnuts, which will come out encased in a transparent amber shell. The process works best in dry (not humid) weather. Use ⅛ teaspoon cream of tartar instead of the soda. Boil until the mixture reaches 234°F on a candy thermometer. Store in a cool, dark place and serve within 6 to 8 hours.

Rubber gloves protect the hands from vegetable and fruit stains; they are especially needed in making grape jelly. Get them several sizes too large or the hand will not have room for free action. Grease will melt them.
— Alice L. James, Catering for Two, Comfort and
  Economy for Small Households, 1898

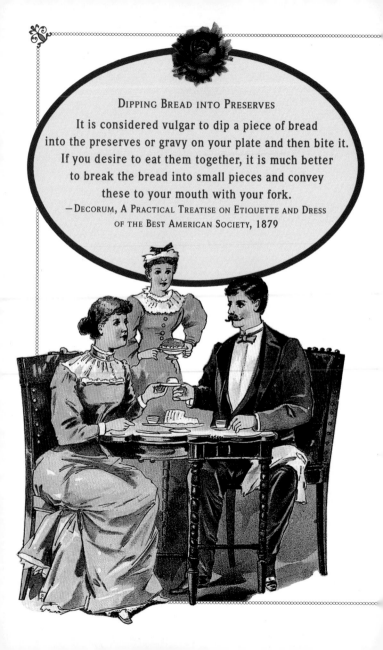

DIPPING BREAD INTO PRESERVES

It is considered vulgar to dip a piece of bread
into the preserves or gravy on your plate and then bite it.
If you desire to eat them together, it is much better
to break the bread into small pieces and convey
these to your mouth with your fork.

—DECORUM, A PRACTICAL TREATISE ON ETIQUETTE AND DRESS
OF THE BEST AMERICAN SOCIETY, 1879

Fruit Glacé

Boil together for half an hour one cupful of granulated sugar, one of water. Dip the point of a skewer in the syrup after it has been boiling the given time, and then in water. If the thread formed breaks off brittle the syrup is done. Have oranges pared, divided into eighths, and wiped free of moisture. Pour part of the hot syrup into a small cup, which keep in boiling water. Take the pieces of orange on the point of a large needle or skewer and dip them in the syrup. Place them on a dish that has been buttered lightly. Grapes, cherries, walnuts, etc., can be prepared in the same way. Care must be taken not to stir the syrup, as that spoils it.

—Maria Parloa,
Miss Parloa's New Cook Book, 1880

NOTE: Glacéed fruit will look as though it is encased in clear glass. Boil the syrup for 45 minutes, or until it reaches 234°F on a candy thermometer. Place the fruit on racks rather than on a buttered dish. Store in a cool, dark, dry place. Serve within 6 to 8 hours.

ICED PINEAPPLE

Select nice fruit, remove the outer shell and eyes. Hold the pineapple by the crown and grate it into a dish; then remove the pineapple into a glass dish, sprinkle a little powdered sugar on same, pour a glass of sherry on it and stand in the refrigerator for two hours and serve cold.

— PATENTED AND IMPROVED METHODS OF PRESERVING AND CANNING FRUITS, VEGETABLES, ETC., ALSO PICKLING FRUITS AND VEGETABLES, 1890

NOTE: Victorian cooks loved this exotic fruit and enjoyed preparing it many different ways. Here, pineapple may be finely chopped rather than grated. Do not use the pineapple core. Sprinkle with ¼ cup powdered sugar, and add ½ cup golden sherry. One medium pineapple makes 2 cups Iced Pineapple.

ICED FRUITS

Take fine bunches of ripe currants on the stalks; dip them in gum arabic or the whites of eggs, well beaten; lay them on a sieve. Sift white sugar over and let them dry. They are very nice for dessert or the tea table. Grapes, cherries or plums may be done in the same way.

—May Perrin Goff, THE HOUSEHOLD OF THE DETROIT FREE PRESS, 1881

NOTE: Although some experts caution against consuming raw egg whites, Iced Fruits make lovely decorations and center-pieces. It is not necessary to sift the sugar; it can simply be sprinkled on dipped fruit. Use 1 egg white and 1 cup sugar for every pound of fruit.

As always use a porcelain-lined kettle, and stir with a silver or wooden spoon—never an iron one. Currants are nice mixed with an equal weight of raspberries, and pears are improved by adding quinces or lemon-peel. If equal quantities of quince and apple are canned together, it will taste as if quinces entirely.
—May Perrin Goff, THE HOUSEHOLD OF THE DETROIT FREE PRESS, 1881

To Brandy All Kinds of Fruit

🐝

To every one pound of fruit take one pound of good granulated sugar, and one-quarter of a pint of good white brandy, and use as follows: First pour over just enough water so sugar will dissolve, then drop in your fruit and allow to boil for five minutes for cherries and berries, and eight minutes for peaches, pears, plums, pineapples and apples, and ten minutes for apricots, crab apples and quinces.

Take out fruit and place in hot jars on back of stove in dripping pan as described in fruit, having cover on jars; boil down the syrup fifteen minutes and pour this syrup over fruit to overflowing and seal. The brandy must never be added until the syrup is boiled down as described.

— Patented and Improved Methods of Preserving and Canning Fruits, Vegetables, etc., Also Pickling Fruits and Vegetables, 1890

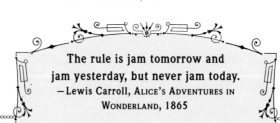

The rule is jam tomorrow and jam yesterday, but never jam today.
—Lewis Carroll, Alice's Adventures in Wonderland, 1865

NOTE: Brandied fruits in decorated jars make lovely holiday gifts. This recipe works well for plums, peaches, cherries, and berries. Prepare jars as directed on page 57. Reduce the cooking time to avoid overcooking. Plums: Cook 4 medium plums (1 pound) in syrup made of 4 cups sugar and 4 cups water (brought to a boil and stirred constantly until sugar is dissolved) for 3 minutes. Place in two pint jars and add 6 tablespoons brandy to each jar. Fill with hot syrup, leaving ¼ inch headspace (not to overflowing). Seal and process for 20 minutes. Peaches: For 4 medium peaches (1 pound), use 4 cups sugar, 4 cups water, and ½ cup brandy. Follow the directions for plums (peaches should be brandied without pits). Cherries and berries (1 pound): Follow the directions for plums, but cook for just 2 minutes.

Pickles

No Victorian lunch or dinner was complete without pickles. Menus in Victorian cookbooks provide endless suggestions: mixed pickle, spiced cucumber pickle, sweet pepper pickle, pickled onions, and pickled cabbage, to name but a few. A meal was apparently unthinkable, if not uneatable, without them. "Next to eating such quantities of cake and pastry, I think Americans are most absurd in their free use of pickles and condiments," wrote Emma P. Ewing in *Cooking and Castle-Building* (1880). M. E. W. Sherwood, in *The Art of Entertaining* (1893), enumerating "unrivalled Amer-

ican delicacies''—Virginia terrapin, gumbo, and crayfish bisque among them—also singled out green pepper pickles and tomato catsup (''a Maryland success''). Olives, pickles, and other relishes, Sherwood continued, were always welcome additions to the table. So great was the love for pickles that they were even recommended as an essential part of a Victorian midnight snack. What could be more appetizing, asked Laura C. Holloway in *The Hearthstone* (1883), than a late-night repast of bread, cheese, and butter, with perhaps a glass of milk and some pickles? Finally, such was the homey connotation of pickles in general that Moses Fagus, writing in the 1880s, titled his magazine column in *The Housekeeper* ''Letters from Pickle Corners.''

During the nineteenth century *pickle* was a less specific term than it is today. Gherkins and other cucumbers were, of course, among the most popular pickled vegetables. ''Many people prefer cucumber pickles, pure and simple, to all mixtures and preparations'' was Emma Ewing's opinion. *The Housekeeper's New Cook Book* (1883) considered cucumbers ''one of the most useful vegetables we have,'' able to be dressed in a greater variety of ways than any other except the tomato.

Generally, however, *pickle* meant any fruit or vegetable steeped in a rather potent combination of vin-

egar, salt, and spices. Just as common as pickled cucumbers were green tomato pickles, pepper pickles, pickled mushrooms, pickled plums, and "India" or "Indian" pickle, a very spicy mix of at least five or six different vegetables — usually cauliflower, gherkins, cabbage, French beans, and onions — soaked in ginger, hot pepper, mustard, and turmeric.

Sweet pickles were a variation on the familiar receipt, with sugar added to the brine. Blueberry pickle, pear pickle, cherry pickle, and gingery pickled melon rind were all prepared in this manner. Sweet tomato pickles, and sweet pickled beets and onions, were also made with this sugary brine. "Sweet pickles are served with game or poultry and are a nice relish," commented *The Ladies' World* (1901) on its

**Pickles are fork foods; it is a mistake
to take them in the fingers.**
—CORRECT SOCIAL USAGE (VOL. 1),
   A COURSE OF INSTRUCTION IN GOOD FORM, STYLE AND
   DEPORTMENT BY EIGHTEEN DISTINGUISHED AUTHORS, 1907

recipe for "very sweet" peach pickles, immersed in
mace, allspice, cinnamon, and sugared cider vinegar.
They were, however, "troublesome to keep and un-
less they are sealed up airtight they should be exam-
ined frequently, and scalded if there are signs of
fermentation."

Proper methods of preparation, utensils, and vinegar-to-spice proportions of the pickling brine were a constant topic of discussion among Victorian cooks. "Avoid bringing anything but wooden spoons, etc., in contact with the vinegar; the vessels used should be lined with porcelain in all cases," advised *The Art of Canning, Pickling, Smoking and Preserving* (n.d.). "Glass jars or wooden kegs are the best receptacles in which to keep pickles. Glazed earthenware jars should never be used under any circumstances, as the acid acting upon the glazing generates a potent poison." (This referred to lead glazes, now banned in the United States for use on ceramics.)

The degree of hotness or sweetness desired in a pickle varied according to taste, hence the great variations in recipes. But nearly every Victorian vegetable or fruit had pickling in its future. According to *The New Cyclopedia of Domestic Economy and Practical Housekeeper* (1872), "As the spring advances, a portion of every small root produced in a garden, if collected and thrown into cold vinegar, till it can be conveniently made into a regular pickle, will be found most excellent, at no greater expense than the cost of the spice and vinegar, and the trouble of mixing it."

Today's cooks can still enjoy the Victorians' clever means of spicing up the everyday fare of the dinner table.

MIXED PICKLE

Take anything that can be pickled, such as onions, sliced cucumbers, cabbage, mangoes, peppers, small green tomatoes, cauliflowers, martinoes, celery, green beans, nasturtiums, watermelon rind, and chili peppers. Lay them in salt and water, with enough turmeric to turn them yellow. Let them stand 24 hours, stirring frequently; then drain and dry them, and put them into jars. To every quart of vinegar allow a tablespoon of mustard seed, one of turmeric, and one of whole black peppers, some garlic if you like. Spice to your taste with mace, cloves, ginger, red pepper and horseradish. Boil all this but the mustard seed in a bag with the vinegar; let it stand till cold. Boil

CUCUMBER
WILD

THE PAGE SEED COMPANY.
GREENE, N.Y.

some eggs quite hard, mash them in enough sweet oil to make a paste; then stir into the vinegar, and pour over the pickles. Put a handful of salt to every jar. Let them stand three days, covered tight, and they will be ready to use.

—Miss T. S. Shute, THE AMERICAN HOUSEWIFE COOKBOOK. PARTS I AND II, 1880

NOTE: This "short-term" pickle is more a marinated salad than a true pickle. Prepare jars as directed on page 57. Use 3 medium onions, 1 large unwaxed cucumber, and 6 small, un-ripe, sliced tomatoes. Cut cucumber into ½-inch thick chunks. Slice onion. Brine them in 8 cups water, 3 tablespoons salt, and 4 tablespoons turmeric. Boil 2 quarts white (distilled) vinegar with a spice bag of ½ teaspoon red pepper flakes, 2 table-spoons turmeric, 2 tablespoons whole black pepper, 6 garlic cloves, 2 teaspoons mace, 2 teaspoons cloves, 1 ½-inch chunk of fresh unpeeled ginger, and ⅓ cup grated horseradish for 1 minute. Let cool. Use 6 eggs, peeled and cooled, and ¼ cup vegetable oil. Spoon the vegetables into the jars. Pour in the vinegar to within ½ inch of the rim. Add ¼ teaspoon salt and ¼ teaspoon yellow mustard seed to each jar. Cover the jars with lids and refrigerate. Mixed Pickle should be ready to use in three days and should be eaten within a week.

Makes 4 quarts.

WATERMELON AND SWEET GINGER PICKLES

Cut watermelon rinds in fancy shapes. Soak in salt and water a week. To eight pounds of rind put five pounds of sugar; make a syrup of vinegar and sugar; spice well. Take the rind from the brine, boil in strong ginger tea; let stand over night and heat again. Take out and drop in the syrup. Seal.

—"Household Topics," THE LADIES' WORLD, 1901

NOTE: Gingery watermelon pickles make a special garnish at luncheon or tea or on a picnic. Prepare jars as directed on page 57. Pare the watermelon and discard the peel and pink flesh, retaining the white rind. Small strips may be substituted for "fancy shapes." Soak the rind in 2 quarts water and ½ cup salt overnight. Drain and rinse the rind. Simmer the rind in 4 cups water and 2 hands (8 ounces) unpeeled ginger for 30 minutes over medium-low heat. Let stand overnight. Boil the rind in a syrup of 8 cups sugar, 3 cups white (distilled) vinegar, 4 cups water, and a spice bag of 2 cinnamon sticks, 3 teaspoons whole cloves, and 3 teaspoons whole allspice. Fill the jars to within ¼ inch of the rim. Seal and process for 10 minutes as directed on pages 56–58. Store in a cool, dark, dry place.

Makes 3 pints.

Sweet pickles may be made of any fruit that can
be preserved including the rind of cucumbers or
melons. The proportions of sugar to vinegar is
three pints to a quart. Make into a syrup and
pour over the ripe fruit. With some fruits it is
necessary that they may be scalded or steamed;
with others it is not. Very ripe peaches or plums
do not need steaming, but pears, apples, cucumber and melon rinds are better steamed and the
hot vinegar syrup afterward poured over them.
With these it is also necessary that the spices
should be put in bags or the fruit will be much
discolored. Crabapples make particularly good
pickles, though many seem to think only of making them into jelly or preserves.

—May Perrin Goff,
THE HOUSEHOLD OF THE DETROIT FREE PRESS, 1881

Tomato Mangoes

Select large, smooth, green tomatoes, cut from the stem end a slice large enough to allow the removal of the seeds without breaking the tomato, then stand in a large pan with the slice cut from the top near each one. Put a teaspoon of salt in each one, cover with cold water and soak for twenty-four hours, drain and fill with a mixture made of two heads of cabbage, chopped fine, one teaspoonful each of ground cloves and allspice, four tablespoons of whole mustard, and two tablespoonfuls of salt. When filled tie the top on each with twine, stand in a stone jar and cover with cold vinegar. Ready for use in one week.

VARIATION: PEPPER MANGOES — Take large green peppers, cut a slit in the sides and remove the seeds, stand in strong salt water for twenty-four hours. Take out and stuff with chopped cabbage seasoned with salt, mustard seed and celery seed. Tie together, place in a jar and cover with good vinegar. Unripe muskmelons may be pickled in the same way and are very nice.

— THE MAYFLOWER, 1899

NOTE: To the Victorians, "mangoes" were not the tropical fruit but a stuffed fruit or vegetable. Use 2 large tomatoes or 3 small green, red, or yellow peppers, 2 cups finely chopped cabbage, ½ teaspoon salt, 1 teaspoon mustard seed, ½ teaspoon celery seed, and 3 cups cider vinegar. Refrigerate for a week. For a less acidic taste, add 1 to 2 tablespoons brown sugar. Mangoes should be eaten within two weeks.

Each stuffed fruit or vegetable makes 1 serving.

Do you know, Emeline, it is said that cloves scattered over any pickle, sweet or sour, will effectually prevent mould?
—Emma P. Ewing, COOKING AND CASTLE-BUILDING, 1880

BLUE-BERRY PICKLES

For blue-berry pickles, old jars which have lost their
covers, or whose edges have been broken so that
the covers will not fit tightly, serve an excellent
purpose, as these pickles must not
be kept airtight.

Pick over your berries, using only sound ones; fill
your jars or wide-mouth bottles to within an inch of
the top, then pour in molasses enough to settle down
in all the spaces; this cannot be done in a moment, as
molasses does not run very freely. Only lazy people
will feel obliged to stand by and watch its progress. As
it settles, pour in more until the berries are covered.
Then tie over the top a place of cotton cloth to keep
the flies and other insects out, and set away in the
preserve closet. Cheap molasses is good enough and
your pickles will soon be "sharp." Wild grapes may
be pickled in the same manner.

—Mrs. F. L. Gillette and Hugo Ziemann,
THE WHITE HOUSE-COOKBOOK, A COMPREHENSIVE
CYCLOPEDIA OF INFORMATION FOR THE HOME, 1887

Scour your pickle and preserve jars after they are
emptied; dry and put them away in a dry place.
—May Perrin Goff, THE HOUSEHOLD OF
THE DETROIT FREE PRESS, 1881

NOTE: Delicious plain or over a simple cake, Blue-Berry Pickles should be eaten within one to two weeks. Prepare jars as directed on page 57. Use 1 cup molasses to ½ pint blueberries. Fill the jars at room temperature, cover with lids, and refrigerate.

Makes 1 pint.

Among pickles, sweet or spiced ones are my favorites, although mamma, no doubt, would object to them as occupying neutral ground between pickles and preserves, as being too undecided, not positive enough, in character to suit her.
—Emma P. Ewing, COOKING AND CASTLE-BUILDING, 1880

SWEET PICKLE FOR FRUIT

(PEACHES, PLUMS, ETC.)

The cling-stone peaches are best for pickling, though
many use the free-stone, as well. Some people peel them,
while others rub the down off with a coarse
towel, and leave the skins on. To

8 lbs of fruit, allow

4 pounds sugar,

1 quart vinegar,

2 ounces of stick cinnamon,

2 ounces of cloves.

Boil the sugar and vinegar with the cinnamon, for five
minutes, then put in the peaches, a few at a time, with
one or two cloves in each peach. When they are done
enough to prick easily with a fork, take them out in
the jar, and put in others to cook, until they have all
been cooked. Boil the syrup down to one half the
original quantity and pour it over the peaches. Seal
while hot.

—Mrs. T. J. Kirkpatrick,
THE HOUSEKEEPER'S NEW COOK BOOK, 1883

NOTE: Sweet pickle made from fruit was traditionally served with game or poultry. Prepare jars as directed on page 57. Use 2 pounds peaches or plums, 4 cups sugar, 2 cups cider vinegar, an 8-inch cinnamon stick, and 12 cloves. Boil for 3 minutes. Fill the jars to within ¼ inch of the rim. Seal and process for 20 minutes as directed on pages 56–58.

Makes 4 pints.

When peaches are extremely scarce and one wishes to utilize every bit possible of them, a delicious confection can be made from the skins; for every quart of parings, allow one cupful of water, cook until very soft, then press gently through a fine sieve, extracting every bit of the pulp. Allow one pound of sugar for every pint of this thick juice, put all together over the fire, and simmer until very thick.

—THE LADIES' WORLD, 1901

Relishes

❧ VICTORIAN RELISHES — FLAVORED CATSUPS AND MUSTARDS, CHUTNEYS, AND CHOWCHOWS, as well as olives, pickles, capers, and celery — were another indispensable part of the nineteenth-century menu. "There is one class of materials in constant use in the kitchen: — the condiments; without these, soups, sauces, and all made dishes, would be insipid; and the judicious application of them is essential," declared *The New Cyclopedia of Domestic Economy and Practical Housekeeper* (1871). *The American Practical Cookery Book, or, Housekeeping Made Easy* (1861) designated these dishes as *kickshaws,* a term meaning appetizers, delicacies, and fancy

dishes. Mary B. Welch in her 1884 cookery guide (*Mrs. Welch's Cook Book*) acknowledged that while these items were not food per se, they were highly valued as adjuncts: "They render the food more palatable, stimulate the appetite, and assist in preserving food."

Ketchups, or catsups, as they were more widely known, were a basic Victorian condiment, available in flavors well beyond today's standard tomato. "Mushrooms are greatly used in domestic cooking, and are a general favorite," one book explained.

Other Victorian favorites were walnut, oyster, apple, lemon, gooseberry, and even peach catsups, all of which could be used to flavor sauces or as savory accompaniments to a meal. Victorians loved the taste combination of salty, savory, and sweet, and regularly doused their meats with even the sweetest of these catsups. *The New Cyclopedia of Domestic Economy and Practical Housekeeper* even offered a recipe for a "7 years catsup" made from strong beer, red wine, shallots, anchovies, mace, nutmeg, ginger, and cloves. The authors noted that it "may be carried on a voyage around the world."

Flavored vinegars—raspberry, elder flower, tarragon, gooseberry, walnut, and others—were also Victorian staples, as were the spicy chowchows and piccalillis. Chutneys gained favor as the British Victorians expanded their empire to India and in turn exported these influences to America. Victorian chefs took inspiration from around the world, and their wholehearted pleasure in variety is reflected in the galaxy of condiments they borrowed and invented.

Relishes are nowhere more acceptable than upon the luncheon table. . .
—Helen Louise Johnson, THE ENTERPRISING HOUSEKEEPER, 1898

KATE'S LILY PICKLE

Chop one gallon of green tomatoes; sprinkle salt over them and let them lie twenty-four hours; drain off the liquor and throw it away; then add twelve onions chopped, six green peppers, three quarts chopped cabbage, one half pint grated horseradish, one half pint white mustard-seed, black pepper, cloves, etc., to taste. Put vinegar to this and cork tight.

—Mrs. Winslow's Domestic Receipt Book for 1865

Note: Cooking the vegetables extends the shelf life of this piccalilli, which can accompany marinated fish or chicken, mix into fresh salads, or make a tangy topping for mild-flavored vegetables, such as potatoes or squash. Prepare jars as directed on page 57. Chop 2 pounds of green tomatoes, 4 medium yellow onions, 2 large green peppers, 4 cups of cabbage, and 1 cauliflower into small pieces. Combine with 2 tablespoons salt, ½ cup grated horseradish, 2 teaspoons yellow mustard seed, 1 teaspoon black pepper, 4 teaspoons brown sugar, 1 teaspoon celery seed, 2 teaspoons black mustard seed, and 2 cups white (distilled) vinegar. Bring to a boil, then reduce the heat to medium-low and simmer, covered, for 1 hour. Fill the jars to within 1 inch of the rim. Seal and process for 15 minutes as directed on pages 56–58.

Makes 8 cups.

PEACH CATSUP

Pare and quarter eight quarts ripe sound peaches. Simmer the parings for half hour in one pint of water. Then strain, add the peaches to the liquor, and simmer half hour longer; add one and a half cupfuls vinegar, half cupful sugar, two teaspoonfuls ground cinnamon, and half teaspoonful each cloves, mace and pepper. Simmer slowly until rather thick and seal hot in pint jars.

— THE LADIES' WORLD, 1901

NOTE: Try this traditional fruity catsup with poultry or lamb. Prepare jars as directed on page 57. Use 5 medium peaches, ⅓ cup water, ¼ cup white (distilled) vinegar, 2 tablespoons sugar, ½ teaspoon cinnamon, and ⅛ teaspoon each cloves, mace, and black pepper. Simmer, uncovered, over medium-low heat for 45 minutes, or until thick. Fill the jars to within ¼ inch of the rim. Seal and process for 10 minutes as directed on pages 56–58.

CHOWCHOW
(Superior English Recipe)

This excellent pickle is seldom made at home, as we can get the imported article so much better than it can be made from the usual recipes. This we vouch for as being as near the genuine article as can be made. One quart of young, tiny cucumbers, not over two inches long, two quarts of very small white onions, two quarts of tender string beans, each one cut in halves, three quarts of green tomatoes, sliced and chopped very coarsely, two fresh heads of cauliflower, cut into small pieces, or two heads of white, hard cabbage.

After preparing these articles, put them in a stone jar, mix them together, sprinkling salt between them sparingly. Let them stand twenty-four hours, then drain off all the brine that has accumulated. Now put these vegetables in a preserving kettle over the fire, sprinkling through them an ounce of turmeric for

ONION
Small Pickling

THE PAGE SEED COMPANY
GREENE, N.Y.

52

coloring, six red peppers, chopped coarsely, four tablespoonfuls of mustard seed, two of celery-seed, two
of whole allspice, two of whole cloves, a coffee cup of
sugar, and two-thirds of a teacup of best ground mustard. Pour on enough of the best cider vinegar to cover
the whole well; cover tightly and simmer all well
until it is cooked all through and seems tender, watch-
ing and stirring it often. Put in bottles or glass jars. It
grows better as it grows older, especially if sealed
when hot.

—Mrs. F. L. Gillette and Hugo Ziemann,
THE WHITE HOUSE COOKBOOK, A COMPREHENSIVE
CYCLOPEDIA OF INFORMATION FOR THE HOME, 1887

NOTE: Victorian recipes for chowchow vary; almost any combination of vegetables can be used. Prepare jars as directed on
page 57. Use 1 medium cauliflower, broken into small pieces; 2
large white onions, chopped; 1 pound of green beans; and ¼
cup kosher salt. A stainless-steel pot may be substituted for
the stone jar. After draining off the brine, add 2 large red
peppers, 2 tablespoons turmeric, 2 tablespoons mustard seed,
1 tablespoon celery seed, 1 tablespoon whole allspice, 1 tablespoon whole cloves, ½ cup sugar, ⅓ cup ground mustard, and 8
cups cider vinegar. Cover the pot. Cook for 30 to 45 minutes, or
until tender. Fill the jars to within ¼ inch of the rim. Seal and
process for 10 minutes as directed on pages 56–58. Store in a
dark, cool, dry place.

Makes 16 cups.

GREEN GRAPE CHUTNEY

Chop one and a half pounds of tart apples and put in a porcelain kettle with two pounds of seeded (green) grapes, four ounces salt, one ounce garlic, one teaspoonful onion juice, one ounce each of grated ginger and horseradish, half teaspoon cayenne, and one pint of vinegar. Cook slowly until reduced to a pulp, turn into a porcelain or earthen vessel, add half pint brown sugar, and stir daily for one week. Put in small jars, seal tightly, and keep in a cool, dry cellar. This is excellent with cold meats.

—"The Housekeeper," THE LADIES' WORLD, 1901

NOTE: As claimed, this tangy chutney is a spicy complement to cold meats. Prepare jars as directed on page 57. Use 1½ pounds Granny Smith apples, 2 pounds green grapes, 1 teaspoon salt, 2 garlic cloves, 1 tablespoon grated fresh ginger, 3 tablespoons grated horseradish, ½ teaspoon cayenne pepper, 1 cup brown sugar, and 2 cups white (distilled) vinegar. Bring to a boil, then reduce the heat to low and simmer, uncovered, for 1½ to 2 hours, or until reduced to a pulp. Chutney should be placed immediately in the jars to within ¼ inch of the rim. Seal and process for 10 minutes as directed on pages 56–58.

Makes 2 pints.

PLUM CATSUP

Wash fruit and take out stones. To five pounds of fruit take three pounds of sugar, a large cupful of vinegar, one large tablespoonful of cloves, one of cinnamon (ground). Mix well and boil one hour.

—"The Housekeeper," THE LADIES' WORLD, 1901

NOTE: Prepare jars as directed on page 57. Use 2½ pounds plums, 3 cups sugar, ½ cup white (distilled) vinegar, 1½ teaspoons cloves, and ½ teaspoon cinnamon. Bring to a boil, covered, over medium heat. After the fruit softens, remove the cover, reduce the heat to low, and, stirring occasionally, simmer for 1 hour, or until thick. Mash the fruit with a potato masher or purée it in a blender until the texture is smooth. Fill the jars with the hot mixture to within ¼ inch of the rim. Seal and process for 10 minutes as directed on pages 56–58.

Makes 3 cups.

PROCESSING AND CANNING

Preparing the recipes in this book is, in a way, intuitive. The best results come from practice and experience — the cook's ability to estimate the proper thickness and to vary timing and ingredients according to the sweetness, tartness, or ripeness of the produce. Preserving and pickling were such common activities for a Victorian rural woman that certain steps needed no explanation. Thus, recipes may seem vague to modern readers. A few suggestions can help to make the preserving process simpler and safer.

The following equipment is essential: canning jars with new lids, a canning kettle with a special canning rack for the jars, and a rubber-reinforced jar lifter, all of which are available in standard cookware stores. The best cookware for canning is unchipped enamelware, stainless steel, or glass. Never use aluminum or iron, which can impart their flavors to the food, or copper, which can react toxically with acidic ingredients. Always use fresh ingredients, and wash produce thoroughly. Bananas, lemons, limes, melons, oranges, and persimmons are not recommended for canning.

Any amount of food can be cooked for canning. The equipment and the food should always be the same temperature. For example, hot mixtures should always be placed in hot jars. To avoid bacteria in the food, which can cause fermentation, mold, and botulism poisoning, all preserves must be immediately processed in a hot-water bath, according to the following directions.

1. Examine the jars for nicks or cracks, and discard the imperfect jars. Wash the jars, bands, and lids in hot, soapy water. Sterilize the jars by boiling them for 15 minutes in a large container (immerse them so they fill with water) or by washing them in a hot dish-washer. The jars should remain in hot water until they are to be used.
2. Sterilize the lids and bands by placing them in barely simmering water for 10 minutes. Do not boil. Remove the pot from the heat, but leave the lids and bands in hot water until they are to be used.
3. Fill the jar with pickle, preserve, or relish, leaving appropriate space between the food and the rim of the

jar (½ inch or ¼ inch for fruits, tomatoes, jams, jellies, marmalades, pickles, and other relishes; ½ inch for vegetables). Remove air bubbles in jams by inserting a rubber spatula or other nonmetallic kitchen utensil between the jar and the food, using it as you would a knife to loosen a cake.

4. Clean any excess preserve from the jar and top, then place the lid on the jar, with the rubber side next to the glass. Firmly screw the band in place.

5. Fill the canning kettle with water to 1 or 2 inches above the jars and bring to a boil. Carefully place the hot jars of pickles or preserves in racks in the kettle.

6. The processing time, which begins once the water returns to a boil, varies according to the type of fruit or vegetable being canned (see chart, page 59). At elevations higher than 3,000 feet, add 2 minutes processing time for each additional 1,000 feet.

7. After processing, place the jars on dry towels or a wooden surface to cool for 12 to 24 hours (never place the jars on a cold surface, because they could crack). Do not retighten the bands. If correctly sealed, the dome in the center of the lid will be down after cooling, rather than up. If the lid fails to seal properly, either reprocess or refrigerate and eat promptly.

8. To prevent rusting, remove the bands after the jars have cooled. If the seal is correctly formed, the lid will have enough suction to be held down indefinitely. Store in a cool, dry, dark spot. Refrigerate after opening.

The Proper Time to Can
Fruits and Vegetables as They
Come in Their Season

Cherries (the Ox Heart are the best)
.... From June 15th to July 1st
Currants and Strawberries .... June 10th to July 1st
Raspberries .... July 1st to July 5th
Blueberries .... July 1st to Aug. 5th
Blackberries .... July 15th to Aug. 25th
Pineapples (Sugar Loaf are best;
    over-ripe will not answer) .... May 10th to July 1st
Peaches (the late Crawfords
    are the best) .... Aug. 20th to Oct. 5th
Pears .... Aug. 20th to Oct. 15th
Apricots and Plums .... Aug. 10th to Sept. 10th
Apples (the Pippin are the best) ... Oct. 20th to Nov. 20th
Quinces .... Sept. 10th to Oct. 25th
Asparagus (the best for canning purposes
    is grown in New Jersey) .... May 15th to July 1st
Peas .... May 25th to July 1st
Tomatos .... Aug. 15th to Oct. 1st
Corn .... Aug. 15th to Oct. 15th
Beans .... Sept. 20th to Oct. 20th
Lima Beans .... Aug. 20th to Oct. 15th
Rhubarb .... May 15th to July 1st
Cauliflower .... Sept. 15th to Oct. 25th

— Patented and Improved Methods of
    Preserving and Canning Fruits, Vegetables, etc.,
    Also Pickling Fruits and Vegetables, 1890

GLOSSARY

BRINE: A strong solution of water and salt used for pickling or preserving foods.

CANDIED FRUIT: Fruit removed from boiling syrup, dried, then dipped in the hot syrup and set to dry again, so a transparent sugar coating is formed.

CATSUP (ALSO CATCHUP OR KETCHUP): A thick, spicy sauce or paste made from vegetables, fruits, or nuts, ranging from walnuts to mangoes to mushrooms to tomatoes, combined with vinegar, sugar, salt, and spices.

CHOWCHOW: A mustard-flavored vegetable-and-pickle relish, originally thought to have been brought to America by Chinese railroad laborers during the nineteenth century.

CHUTNEY: A condiment, ranging from smooth to chunky, in which a variety of fruit is cooked with sugar, vinegar, and spices. Although frequently used to accompany Indian curry dishes, sweeter chutneys are also enjoyed as spreads or with cheese.

COMPOTE: A whole cooked preserved fruit, usually brandied and served in its own syrup.

CONFITURE: Jam or preserves.

CRYSTALLIZED FRUIT: Fruit removed from boiling syrup, then rolled in sugar and left to dry.

FROSTED FRUIT: Fruit dipped in beaten egg white, then dipped in sugar repeatedly until a thick coating is formed.

GLACÉED FRUIT: Candied fruit.

ICED FRUIT: Candied fruit or Frosted fruit.

JAM: A thick, spreadable mixture of fruit, sugar, and often pectin in which whole pieces of fruit or the pulp is cooked until soft. Jam is usually made of juicy berries, such as strawberries, raspberries, currants, and mulberries.

JELLY: A clear spread prepared with the juices of fruit boiled with an equal quantity of sugar. Fruits such as apples, gooseberries, quinces, Seville oranges, red currants, and others that naturally contain large amounts of pectin usually make the best jellies.

MARMALADE: A clear spread best described as a jelly in which pieces of fruit and fruit rind are suspended. The term is usually applied to those spreads made of citrus fruits and rinds, or firm fruits such as pineapple.

PICCALILLI: A highly seasoned, spicy pickled vegetable relish, usually chopped, used as an accompaniment to another dish.

PICKLES: Vegetables or fruits that have been preserved in a seasoned vinegar mixture or brine. They can be sour, sweet, hot, or otherwise flavored.

PRESERVES: Whole or large pieces of fruit cooked with sugar in a syrupy base. Preserves generally are chunkier than jam. According to the venerable Isabella Beeton in *Beeton's Book of Household Management,* there are two kinds of preserved fruits, wet and dry. Wet are kept in their syrup; dry are crystallized or frosted with sugar.

RELISH: A highly seasoned sauce like catsup or mustard, or a zesty seasoned vegetable or fruit condiment.

SYRUP: Varying proportions of sugar and water heated together to preserve the aroma and flavor of the fruit.

A great blessing has been gained by the development of the various methods of preserving fruits in such a manner as to retain their juices, salts, and flavor.

—Mary B. Welch,
MRS. WELCH'S COOK
BOOK, 1884